WAVES OF HEART

AN ANTHOLOGY OF SHORT POEMS

SARATH KUMAR KALAMATA

ISBN 979-888530567-9

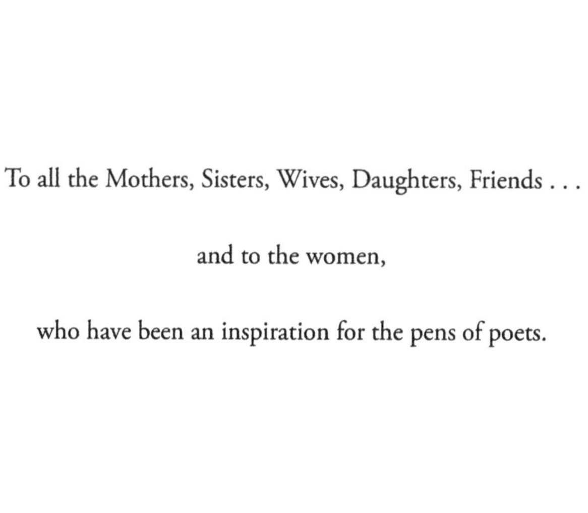

To all the Mothers, Sisters, Wives, Daughters, Friends . . .

and to the women,

who have been an inspiration for the pens of poets.

Contents

Contents

Contents

Foreword

The Book "Waves of Heart" is a poetry collection. In life, during different stages, people encounter each emotion with variable intensities. When I wrote these poems, I was a college student. Most of them were just chaos running in an imbalance mind.

Here I categorised the poems into several parts which include Love Poems, Heart Break Poems, Poems on Self and Other Poems. Each category has some loud thoughts that I wanted to share with the world and inspired from many things.

While reading this book and the poems in it, if you're touched by those words, I feel blessed in a way. Afterall, my poetry maybe an art but art can change the world. I believe in this line, as I'm an example of a changed person.

Sometimes I was lost in thoughts.
But when I pen them down, only a few take form in this book.
The others were still lost . . .

Preface

The idea of this Book just hit my mind during my college days. I used to write poetry for a hobby and with a few admirers the hobby turned into social media attention seeker. And with all the inspiration and support, the book finally got a face.

In this book, most poems are written as a diary note as to be read by the writer alone. Embarrassed, I was a bit shy to open up my works to the world. After a lot of struggle and love for poetry, I wanted to let the world learn the little secret of my scrap note.

The final collection I named as The Waves of Heart.

Acknowledgements

How can I say thanks in just words? I have a lot of them to name here.

Firstly, my god Shiva, for blessing me in uncountable ways.

I would like to thank my Mother who had thaught and inspired me to learn and feel the world.

My Teachers who made me fall in love with Poetry and Language.

My Friends who allowed me to see life in a different perspective and shared moments.

The women in the stories/poems of many poets, poetesses, story writers, movies and paintings.

The imaginary girl who is the theme of many poems that was written in this book.

Poems on Nature

Some poems are inspired from the nature we live in. And a few of them are in the next pages.

1. Painfully Beautiful

She used to fall in love
with souls of nature.
Moon, sang her lullaby
Wind was her messenger
the fire, the water and the thunder
were her friends to share a game.
When she found love in a person
the nature lost its soulmate.
Water left her as a tear
Wind from her Nostrils
Fire, hidden in the darkness.
While the moon sang her songs
her eyes held poetry within.
It was a beautiful story;
So painfully beautiful. . .

2. Sky Drops

The drops twinkle in the sky,
falling down. . . .
They touch me,
when I am along their way to earth.
In the journey, they seem to be like jewels.
Splitting themselves to collect the joyful splashes.
Beyond the age,
Enjoy the breeze.
It's just a magic of nature freezing us a moment.

3. You are a Drop

You have been a drop, as always
Soaked in the sky, sunken in the cloud
Hanging like a star
Blazing like the diamond
When the sun ray pierces your heart.
It is a sea of instincts
Running down with bliss
Into the harsh world.
Your realm is a sign of hope
For an eternity of life
Of appetite, of happiness.
Just, you are a drop
Of life, taken from the heavens
Shared among the widest of mankind.
Just, you are a drop
Quenching the thirst of a million
Spread off with the tear of a billion.
Into the mountains and valleys
Running off, conquering the land.
Like the queen of untamed nature
Dancing all the way you open.

Poems on Self Love

Inspite of everything we love in our lives, the love for one self is mostly unnoticed. We all love ourselves but deny the fact that being selfish saves us a lot of times. Also, being happy is a by-product of being selfish.

The Love we offer others is also a kind of selfishness. We want the other person to love us like we love them. As we expect to be loved, we resist the reality of expecting to be loved as we express.

Some poems on love for one self . . .

4. Battle

With all the hope in the World
That filled my raging heart
I was boosted to fight
A fierce battle with the man
Within me deep inside.
Unknown power that crushes me
Into the sands of dark.
Agony of pain and failure teaches me
Every time when we meet.
But when my dreams take shape
The sleep runs away.
A battle with the dust
Believing it's difficult but not Impossible
When I won, I jumped in Joy.
Still, the sky above continued to Cry.

5. I

I'm a traveler, My Friend
In search of Solitude, I began.
Tasted the ashes of pain,
Blossoms of joy but yet,
Unsatisfied with this stubborn world.
Like a river, I run
I conquer everywhere I flow.
Few lands hurt me and other haunts.
Few hug me, others hide.
But nothing can surpass my journey.
From the stillness of Deserts
To the burning soil under my feet,
From the chillness of Ice,
To the melting glaciers around,
I flow and flow and flow.
Until I dry and die...

6. My Journey

Streaming down like water in a lake,
With all ups and downs, I conquer . . .
the Throne of my Life.
It's an aimless victory. . . .
that suspects the joys in the land
far away from my sight. . .
Not knowing where to go and where not to.,
I have my journey,
Through the hard rocks of Life,
Having a Pleasure of enjoyment,
To have it throughout my journey. . .

7. Like a Hidden Demon

Like a hidden demon
I was left untouched, untamed, unspoiled
by the emotional utterances held by the clutches of sorrow.
My soul was pure as the tears of a cursed lover.
My life left as an open book full of hidden secrets.
A glory for an eternity arisen under the dark side of the moon.
Pain is far away forbidding the touch of my cruelty.
The heights roll down with tastes of salt, like a bitter memory.
Grave speaks of illness of mind to bother the glowing light.
Brother! I'm doomed to be a rock at heart,
Take my steps into the course of kindness from the hell.

8. Me or My Poetry

Choose my poetry over me
because I'm discrete, away from pen.
My real self is a blend,
Inspired by various realms of mankind.
I'm a book in the secret library
with the touch of emotions
that i submerge within me,
while the journey spills around.
And you can find very few of them
in my words that touch your soul.
I may hurt you with my naked self
like the thorn on the stem of a red rose
but my poetry will always inspire you
to become someone better and influencing.
Choose my poetry over me
because I'm a secret
but my work always resembles my heart.

9. A Proposal

It's the best twilight within my past.
Birds turning off to their homes,
I was into bask of the Evening,
To my tired lids, twinklings splashed
Before me in the form of a Damsel.
Her eyes were blue like the sky.
Missing balance in her innocent looks,
Over the free air, I felt her dancing hair.
The red dimpled cheeks hidden into shy
Lips bitten by tooth, to show her remorse face.
"Had the moon disguised as this pretty one?"
The answer, that I couldn't find!!!
A sudden tone out of her pouty lips;
Meant to be there for me as LOVE.
Cracked into joy, she showed off and turned back.
Confused to her, what's my Answer?
After a battle within, I screwed up
My mind and just defended,
"I was already in a Serious Relationship With. . ."
She left letting me not to finish my words. . .
"Freedom!!!"

10. Shadow in Darkness

In the simmering solitude
When there is no one to share a word
I rest upon my own lap
And was always there to hear
The unspoken voices.
I pulled out the phrases
That were buried deep
Into the unseen and untouched regions
I sometimes named hell.
And you ask me why
My poetry touches your soul????
Bcoz they are the not just poems,
My friend!!!
They are stanzas inked from my ashes
And you read them for mere pleasure.

11. The Depth

My Heart!
You have your reasons.
Like every wave turns into tide
And devotion into a demon,
I wish you to be an Ocean.
Hiding a million memories
And yet, brave on the outside.
Calm and peaceful to eyes
Dangerous and demonic behind them.
Caring like a mother,
Every son finds a pearl of fortune.
Sharing like a Friend,
Every secret safe in your depths.
Loving like an infant,
Every touch, intimates fun.
Moments never gone wasted
In your lap and in a clap,
I rejoice being with you.
My Heart or An Ocean,
Both seem the same.

12. Life's journey

The petrichor running into the aroma of my breath.
every moment of ours I treasured in my heart.
as the cloud growing dark above the eyes,
the sad sky began to cry with its tender tears.
Wind passed by plucking out the warmness,
as the shattered sun hide its presence.
drops touching my face
showering all over my body
slowly made me a kid
dancing in the rain
memories flushed out
life goes on and on and on.

13. A Poet

I fill pages with words
to inspire the silent worlds
And yet, fail to find
an aspiringly beautiful mind
All to the sorrow and grief
I share with its words in brief.
Long live the poet, I cry
Deep down, my pen leaves me dry.
Here I find your smile
Enchanted into poems I pile.
And your only presence
fills my words with essence.
I am a writer to the world
And you, the joy I secretly fold.

14. Secret of a Night

My thirst begins when the sun sinks into shadows.
This blanket of twinkling stars empowers the rage of my famine.
In search of an Amazed Heart, my journey steps ahead.
For mine, an Unconquerable Dream that always keeps me awake.

As I move from step to step, door to door,
Silence holding the voice tighter in its grip, squeezes.
The aroma of warm flood enters my nostrils
Just then, captain of my soul urges to taste the flood.

In the night's deserted stillness, under the blazing red moon
Comes to the border of sleep, a quest for quenching
A hanker, that's never fulfilled, a desire that never finds its appetite.
Until time has grown for sun's bright glare.

Unleashing the monster resting inside, eyes burning red.
Holding a prey into clutches of death, shouts of hunger
Running into streets of silent nights, cut the canines
Deep into her neck and suck from the deepest vein.

Tonight I was quenched
Tomorrow in the silver rains of moon
I raise as the monster passion for blood again.
Fear me, for I'm the devil's blood under the skin.

It's a vampire's secret story.

15. Stranger in my Mirror

I compete with you
And the gaze never leaves
For I need to understand
Who's the best of us.
I maybe real
And you maybe mine
In the mirror against me
But I feel the soul
Not just the beauty
While you strive
For my reflection
And not my character
After all you live for a moment
When I present myself at the mirror
Finally you're so beautiful
That's because I'm the best of myself.

16. Unknown Companion

As I left a few steps away from my stay,
My heart pondered harder as it vomit blood.
The tenderness in its beat had vanished oozing fear.
And the boldness of my speech hidden in a dumb noise.
Every voice running in my thoughts, at a glance left pale.
I felt it like a dream hovering in my memories.
Like an invisible companion forever resting in my mind.
The waving wind left my hair dancing to its rhythm.
Yet, no picture of a sound was seen around.
I was unaware of the province as Real or a Vagary.
Hope it's just happening while I was in the hugs of my bed.
Time was racing with my heart.
Dying to keep itself safe from the stillness of death.
Much more if its blood could touch all the instruments within.
I could sense every single little organ in my body, now.
Still the petrichor was sweet and its aroma;
filling my lungs, that was grasping everything, with the eyes closed.
To the thunderbolt, I can sense the hold of my heart
stunned to the heaviness in the strike.
My fear levels ran through the peaks
finding emptiness of the scene in the dark.

While lightening all over the way filled my eardrums with a beep.
Until I cross the current pole far away from my home,
which dissolves into the free breeze.
The bright light hanging at the top like a corpse,
sighing with a dead look into my frightened eye.
My steps were haunted by an unknown companion
who was pushed away by the flash of the pole.

17. Watcher

I'm a lover of things
and most of the times, I just watch.
I watch entities born
And turn down to ashes
I watch great men being made
until their glory rises
like spilled ink over a calico
And I watch the same men
Tortured and butchered like animals.
I'm still there watching'em all
in tears and blood that oozes
And I've been always Unspoiled
to their cries and there I am
endlessly watching.

18. Writer's Curse

It’s a writer’s curse
that his pain is read
by the entire world
but never understood
It’s a writer’s curse
That the prin is praised
But never felt.
It’s a writer’s curse
to feel things so deeply
creating a masterpiece
out of his aching heart

Love Poems

Love - the most beautiful thing a writer can ever believe in. May it be the love for a person or love for a thing. Here I share my love for the person who is created from various book, movies and thoughts.

I strongly hope for the person of my poems to be somewhere on this earth.

If so, I really wanto meet her.

19. A Salacious Soul

She hit the wall
and broke the resonance
As he sprang upon her flesh
she had nowhere to step away
Beginning from her nude eyes
travelling betwixt her breasts,
he gingerly slid his tongue
kissing every inch of the skin
It was new that night
the fire erupted like a volcano
The rains couldn't quench it
only their wetness did.

20. Turn on

The moment that passes away
Filling my heart with enormous joy.
A moment in my weakest instinct
But yet a desire unleashed out,
Taking out the phoenix raging.
His lips sucking the passion from mine
While I with hold his neck.
I can feel his body against mine
But my tongue touching his'.
Eyes kissing his glance ooze a shy
And I couldn't search a hole
To hide my face with full of blush.
It was more than just a kiss
Two souls playing with each other.
I'm just a typical kind of girl
Graving all my emotional gut
Within the eyebrow steps of my face
A gesture of care and love
Is everything that turns my heart ON.
But this, a bit of music
And a drop of wine, turned my body ON.

21. Art

I'm an artist
She was never complete without me.
Because, she was my best art.
Like tears leaving my eyes,
She was deserted into the greatest of fantasies.
Forever, the art was left, unfinished.
Like a Dream

22. Celebration of Love

I wish you were the moon
Hiding your face in the nakedness of the night.
Together while we swim
In the ocean of clouds and stars for an eternity
The wind touches our bodies
Filling itself with our stories of love
Spreading all over the places with its fragrance
And the night, hiding us as its toy
As we forget the time in each other's hugs.
Here we lay in the deepest of the darkness
Exploring each other, at places unseen,
Moment unforgotten and touches unsaid.
As your thighs get wetter with the pour
My hands playing with your raised beauties
As you take me in to the deepness
I surrounded myself with your moans.
Here we lay while the moon hides it's face
As I dig deeper into your secrets.

23. I Love You

I Love You!! Dear One.
Love you like the way no one else does.
Over the years that passed by
Various things that caught my heart.
Everything was unique like you sway.
Your smile, your voice, your breath,
Overwhelming childishness while you speak.
Unique is the nature that drew me towards.
Mine is a lonely life scattered
Ultimately finding its course to settle down
Never it's finished or restless.
Neither its along nor alone.
You're not a vacation to move on.
You are but a home, to Dwell
And it's just another day…

24. Life and Beyond

I'm jealous of the nature around
While it overwhelms you in most ways.
As the sun touches your ravishing skin,
The wind playing with your flowing hair
The moon watching you dream
The stars hugging you like a blanket
The soil kissing your feet.
I'm jealous when you captivate me
Into your eyes with a wink
While I fight with your aversion
I lose every battle even when I win.
A storm that floods away all my pains
In moment I look at your hazel glance.
This is everything worth fighting for.
My normal days are gone beyond counting
Your magic had stripped me of all solitude.
Your hugs, my home of love and care
Your touch, a blink in divinity and holiness
Your love, nothing to replaced it with.
I'm into the cave of secrets,
For every sin we commit, makes us a little closer.

25. Love Stories

Everytime when I looked
The perpetual sky grinned.
While it twinkled a star
the full moon waved at me
As it swam in the sea of mists.

Few falling stars like mermaids
Shading excellence to the night.
All I knew was those minutes
We spent together recounting these stories.
And now, you are so far away from me
like the bright sun hating a dull sky.
And endlessly, I'm waiting for you
With every one of our stories to be shared.
Ones again, until forever ends.

26. Madness

When you left me
There's an unfilled void
Unknown to anyone around.
My heart broken into pieces
But every piece is an art.
In the words I write,
And the colors I spill,
They mark your essence.
People named it madness
And I answered with a question,
If it isn't madness, how can it be LOVE?

27. My Girl

As days bled into years
And moments into memories
I felt like falling into despair.
Pretty she was, to my eyes
Just as a princess in my books.
And her dignity is something
that was outrageously Attractive.
The time together lasted forever
in my stories that never die.
She was a fearless damsel
and it was my distraction.
I was never a whole
Without her soul.
And now, into the solemn silence
I dwell unrefined.

28. Second Chance

It was the first day at college
As I entered my classroom
with a new hope of future
my eyes caught up to her.
A spark that turned into wild fire,
as the same eyes that I missed
for years were looking at me
and pushing again into the abyss.
Since the last time, I couldn't climb
and yet another push into the dark,
I saw her standing there
behind the crowd hiding herself
from the eyes of people around
with an innocent pale face.
And I stepped towards
as the wind from her pulled me
giving a second chance to win.
Maybe I didn't lose her then,
It might be an opportunity to build
a lover within me to love her more.

29. Sravya

Stars twinkle when you look into my Eyes.
Rosy lips whispering the sound of my name
Air moving around you, dancing with your hair
Very much spoiled in your thoughts that kill my dreams
Youthful and ravishing are you, stole my heart
Aroma of your body, entering my nostrils.
The time watching you dream is so divine
like my love for you. Love you, My Dear…

30. The Perfect Couple

She was bold and beautiful.
I was calm and cultivative.
Together we are the best and brisky.
The fire within, turns her wild
While I count my steps along the beach.
She dances to the music with a bliss
As I turn pages filling them with words.
Two different worlds we are
Like ink and paper.
And so meaningless without each other.
My heart races with the breezing wind
While her's, with the blazing sun.
At times, I'm somewhere, everywhere
And nowhere at ones while she strives
To engulf the universe within her palms.
I'm the poet in my life
And she, my best poem.

Poems on women

Women - The reason for our birth, the beauty we worship and the love we earn.

There are women who were an inspiration for great warriors, cause fo great art and reason for devastation.

I dedicate the following poems to those women who were
our mothers
our sisters
our daughters and
our friends.

31. Mermaid

She sank in my memories
like an untamed and unspoiled heart
beats into the freedom for art.
Moving like waves over the surface
of ocean, trying to kiss the sky,
one moment ceased for the dreams
to flow down and touch the ground.
Until the shore shines with pearls
and left untouched as the horizon far away.
May the storms come and go
May the tides rise and fall
But memories, remain forever
Like a scar on the unbent blade.
She sunk in my memories,
And swam like a mermaid
Left me here, alone in the mere.

32. Brightness

Every tear she shed
Fueled her passion.
Touching the phoenix hidden inside her.
For the fire within, raged
Conquering the sky
Burning every obstacle into ashes,
And the fire in her, lit my soul.

33. Eternal

She is just like her
with unbound compassion
turned into a piercing blade.
In the way she strives for life
taking on the moments of grief.
In tears, she sheds of joy and pain.
In glory, she confines herself
Everything she reminds me of, is her.
The hows, she answers in a blink
the whys, she conquers with a word.
What else a woman like her deserves
other than care and respect
for a lifetime and an eternity.
She is just like her
reminding me of my beloved mother!!!

34. Fallen Stars

Her feet were kissed
by the shore's sand
as the waves touched them.
She laughed like a child
when the sand under her feeth
slipped down with the sed.
And for every shell she collected
they felt like they're the stars
fallen down for her.
As they got into her hands,
they wished to be held
for a bit longer.

35. Fireworks

I turned to a child
while walking in the rain
Holding your warm hand
that soothe me in grief
Lift me while falling apart
caress me in fear.
And I feel you in moments
that I just save for ever.
And I can hear thunder
when I sleep holding you.
Babe, you're a firework.

36. Her eyes

She had peculiarly beautiful eyes
and yes they had a sparkle
but there was something about them,
they are deeper than an ocean.
they can pull you in.
soulfully, they have seen more
pain than most of other.
But they were the eyes
that can see your soul
behind the skin and bones.
maybe they can pierce the heart

37. Like a Diamond

Sun found her hidden
Inside a blanket, dreaming
Of a life she once lived,
From the window pumping
A new day into her new life.
The scars have faded but
Pain, never forgotten.
She rose up as an eagle
Jumping into the infinite sky.
Every step she furthered
Into the world, she taught
them a dangerous habit.
Dealing with her, better
than the past that dwell
in a memory inside heads.
Maybe innocence left her
like water leaving a pond
in a summer's scorch.
But deep down, within the banks
of her soul, she wept until
her eyes burn into pain.
She's been broken.
But beautifully, like a diamond.

38. Naked

She wished to be naked
before him.
Peeling one by one,
She undressed her pain, doubt
and hurts.
When she was totally
released from her covers,
He felt the emerging butterfly
she was unaware of being.
He took her like a precious
stone, with a divine grace
That started to sprout as an
unbound courage.

39. She

She was mad
And it fueled my soul.
Like nothing around her
She ignored the world
And continued to burn
In her own darkness,
That enchanted my senses.
She crafted her world
From ashes of her tears.
Like a phoenix she rose,
From dead and lifeless
To something unfathomable.
She was a dream to many
While a desire to few
And love, she's always been.

40. Silence

The moments you catch me
In your eyes that whisper
A silence into my heart,
They are my memories.
She was rain to be held
And a fire to be loved.
She gossips with her eyes
Like Thunder speaks
With the lightening.
Knowing her is a hunt
For light in the shadow.
And loving, is a war.
You may win or lose
Either way it's a surrender.
To her silence.

41. Sulochana

I live in a world
Where the Smile is only a Gesture
A handshake is only an action.
Words lose their essence.
Belonged to my Routine Day
On my way to the Work
Waiting a short glimpse of around
Still for a few more to pass
A flash struck my sight
Like a tiny thunder into dark
Pulling my heart out of its dwell
Damn! its a Damsel gazing into mine
Her twinkling Eyes; probably
The most beautiful twins I'd ever seen
Plunging into my heart;
Breaking it as if a kid does.
The new born baby staring,
Like the innocent girl waiting
The calm and pleasant wind blowing
You make my heart beating. . .

42. That Woman

With the brightness of her smile
The day had finished it's course
In her, we find a family to love
Not just a person to be with
Everything a boy desires
Was wrapped up like a damsel
Let it be happiness or call it luck
She's the most beautiful flower
In the garden, never to pluck
She's the friend in need
A companion of every deed
Love, tiny word to describe her.
Call her an angel
For her place isn't here
But in hearts that worship.

43. Artist

when i met her,
She was a broken mirror,
A fallen angel and an unfinished art.
With her touch,
she led me into a thousand lives.
To paint her with the rainbow
to unleash the masterpiece
and to walk with her
through the greatest
adventures one can never imagine.
And when she left,
I saw myself as nothing
but an unfinished poem
She made me an art
that I fell in love with
not for a moment but
for several lifetimes.

44. Broken Piece

As the day began its course
She welcomed the ray kissing her.
The scars were no more the same
Tearing the innocence of hers.
While she stepped into the world
Eyes hit her like the rain drops falling
But she had an invisible shield
Inside her, an overwhelming anxiety.
No more, she could take it.
Every time she looked into a mirror,
A pride which raised her eyebrow.
She was broken
With the words, looks and the world.
She was perfectly broken
To cut down the obstacles with the sharp edge.
She is a woman now
Not to the looks, but to the Heart.
A perfectly broken Woman!!

45. The Thunder

She was just beside me
As a thunder, she passed in a blink
But the impact was ever lasting
Every moment, with her in my sight
My life seems so bright.
Her smile, her tone, her bliss
was everything now that I miss.
Maybe she was made only for me!!
It's been years, I never felt the same
But now, into my emptiness,
She pushed herself, with so much…
That I felt her, like a thunder
Touching the Darkest of Nights.

46. Your Earrings

Like the stars
Hanging under the sky
I saw a twinkle
Beside your cheek.
Like a diamond
In the crimson.
Dancing with the movements
As you look around
With a tiny glimpse.
Swallowing all the looks
Into it, like the whirlpool.
I found my heart, lost
And you, gone with a smile.
All the hearts in a collection
Along the side of your earrings.

Breakup Poems

As Galelio said, "At the touch of Love, everyone can become a poet".

If a poet's heart breaks. The results are masterpieces.

47. Days counting. . .

You're the reason
for hope, I'm still alive,
while my broken heart
strives to cease.
You're the treason
for I lost the hope
in everything
that we shared once.
Like the falling season
I was struck here
in your thoughts
and dreams.
Every day I fight
an invisible war within.
Only time heals now
both my heart and my liver.

48. I'm no more your's; my girl

It's the darkest night, that ever i had remembered,
You left me there; In-front of the ocean of tears;
Even i feel the sky, sharing my pain.
It weeps and the salt of the tears touch my lips.
In a night, that is ruling the moon, a
Great Fight in my Heart, to struggle the truth
I'm no more Yours; My Girl. . .
You share the bright, from the moon
Shining like the sun to my eyes.
The angel wishes to be you,
Maybe, they look like you.
The greatest gift i had ever had is you.
You ruined my isolated world and still
I'm no more Yours; My Girl. . .
You showed the heaven, where you lived,
At a glance, you flew off.
Apart from my drowsy eyes,
You made the day, a glorious one.
Your army lead, this single man
To be the King, with you beside and now
I'm no more Yours; My Girl. . .

You left me, you remember?!
It was cold, as your touch,
It was terrific, as you farewell,
It was dark, as you were absent,
It was storming, as i cry,
It was alone, as. . .
I'm no more Yours; My Girl. . .

49. Life and Death

Her smile captured in my memories,
her voice, in my heartbeat;
I knew love at her touch
and pain, when she left.
She's my teacher, at times
taught me to love and die at ones.
Days with her, were my best
Now, everything ceased at rest.
Happy was she, with someone else
And here I strive for her tales
Love made me a writer
Until I died every day for her.
But she's always alive in my words.

50. Loss of Beloved

She had clung to my dreams, like a flower on its branch
Every moment I shared with her, now blur like a memory
The past was hanging like a moonless night, over an utter silence
All that's been mine, Was now left into ashes of sorrow.
When I was effete under her loss, Insipid alike the autumn
My eminence has fallen, akin to the dead petals evading the tree
Thoughts were struck in the heart, resembling a cursing dagger
Driving the life from every nerve, that run away from its debt.

51. Search

In the pages of my book
My search for you never dies.
In every fragrance i breath
I sought for your essence.
My hope for a tomorrow
with you, is what i live for.
The void you left
isn't for anyone to fill.
Maybe, you're remembered
as a finished chapter,
but in my book, every page
that holds your name,
is a story i read again and again.
And my love for you,
is something that i carry
till, my grave and beyond.

52. Sorry

A broken heart of mine
Playfully united in your hands
Showering a mist with love and care
Until I arose to be a kid in the hugs.
The good time like the closeness
Passed away leaving nothing
But memories, sweet and alone.
My voices flow in the apology
For resistance that I offered
While you tried to build a bridge.
And now you show every ache
That killed all our dreams
That were piled up in your thoughts.
And I'm sorry for everything
That was done with or without
A glimpse of reluctance.
The only words that I can offer…
Love you and Sorry.
This might cover up everything
From my side, now. Dear.

53. Tear of Sorrow

The thick darkness around
Haunts me like a wandering ghost.
In the wait, the loneliness lies
As my only companion in joy and grief.
Every drop that the sky vomit,
Cuts off my skin leaving a mark
Of vagary and sorry, like my eyes
Drop a tear of feelings, filled of you.
Every pulse of sound oozing out
My heart speaks only to yours
In a disguise, that none else but you
Can touch or feel its naked tone.
The thunder like a shout
Frightens me with all its might.
Only a few drops of sorrow, that's left
Flow and collect at the edge, in huge.
In a world, that's been dipped in pain,
Washes off its beauty in the drain.
To me, everywhere I feel the touch
Of yours, like a dream and mystery.

54. The Broken Heart

Some people are really a memory.
Just their thought makes your lips stretch.
Even minutes of their presence paints you joys.
Seconds of their sight beautifies your day.
Hours of wait is just gone under relief with their smile.
Years of pain reminds us their loss.
Yet, the memory strikes through the heart.
The Broken Heart!!

55. The Day

I start my day with tears
And end it in the flood.
How do I deny the love
You build in your heart, for me.
We are still in it as it hurts
Like the fire in hell, burning inside.
And I was left with smiles
On my face and pain in my heart
A bitter sweet and the sweetest pain
Of missing you for a lifetime and more

56. The Love

No desire for your beauty,
But always was starving for
A Kingdom in your Heart.
Maybe now, I found it
Deep inside; hidden, unseen.
Like the glow of a New Moon.
Steaming all my blood in the veins,
Sucking the life, out of my heart,
Drowning in the ocean of Love;
Unknown tides rise up and fall down,
Unnamed forces tear me apart,
Like currents running into water
Deep inside, I can taste the Love.
The Love, I was always thirst for;
The Love, You always hide from me;
The Love, you're unaware of having with you;
The Love, which was forbidden from giving;
Into the depth of dark mysteries,
I travel long long and long away;
Holding on, to my memories in the basket;
The carrier, for all collections of thoughts.
The memories were only from you;
As a gift, for a child,

You presented with your presence in me.
Those thoughts can never be restored,
And were only left inside the dark
Patches of smile over my Broken Heart.
This is a poem, of Love.
A love, being dead for insane;
A lover, killed in the most brutal way;
A lover, hidden of being loved
In all the best forms of,
The world's best thing;
THE LOVE

57. The Secret Book

She found a book
Deep in the library of his Heart.
Hidden and Untouched by many
who were just a visitor.
Each chapter is a Day
That she spent with him.
Reminding of his rainbow smile.
Every page is a Road,
That they walked together
With their hearts cling to the other.
And every word is a Kiss,
He saved to present her
Along with the first daylight.
And Ink filling the Pages, resembles
Blood flowing in the river of Sorrows.
In the journey
He made every moment, a memory,
That she forgot in the battle of life.

58. Weakness

I held my pen
in a chilling winter night
to give birth to the poem,
that I kept for years.
Unfinished and yet beautiful
like the cresent moon
In the journey to the paper,
it released an emdless flow of tears
I could call them memories but
you called them weakness.
Afterall my love for you
is my greatest weakness.

59. Time

It's been time
That passes while it pulls.
Leaving à scent on my shirt
Cigarette smoke in my lungs
whiskey drop on my lips
And your touch on my skin,
All I could remember was
Those good old days
when I used to laugh my heart.
Now I remember
And cry in loss of love.
only time reminds
That it's only the time
That remembers.

60. You're my essence

As a poet, I prepare
for answers about my first love
and every word said the same,
I never had the first.
No one ever knew me
Or the one who's behind me.
Every verse and every rhyme
had your essence filled in.
And my love for you
isn't done in one poem,
But in everything
that my pen spills out.
Because,
you've pulled out
the BEST in me.

Final Word

This is the first book from The Waves Of Heart Title. I wish I could publish more books with the series to continue.

If I write poems or stories worth the reader's time, I will definitely publish the next book in the coming days.

I wish Lord Shiva bless me to step ahead.

Har Har Mahadev

Har Har Mahadev

Har Har Mahadev

9 798885 305679

Printed by Libri Plureos GmbH in Hamburg,
Germany